11/11

# ASTRONAUTS

eXtreme jobs

Sarah Tieck

Big Buddy BOOKS
Extreme Jobs

ABDO
Publishing Company

## VISIT US AT
**www.abdopublishing.com**

Published by ABDO Publishing Company, 8000 West 78th Street, Edina, Minnesota 55439.

Copyright © 2012 by Abdo Consulting Group, Inc. International copyrights reserved in all countries. No part of this book may be reproduced in any form without written permission from the publisher. Big Buddy Books™ is a trademark and logo of ABDO Publishing Company.

Printed in the United States of America, North Mankato, Minnesota.
062011
092011

♻ PRINTED ON RECYCLED PAPER

Coordinating Series Editor: Rochelle Baltzer
Contributing Editors: Megan M. Gunderson, BreAnn Rumsch, Marcia Zappa
Graphic Design: Marcia Zappa
Cover Photograph: *NASA*.
Interior Photographs/Illustrations: *AP Photo*: AP Photo (p. 25), HO (p. 25), ITAR-TASS (p. 25), Dmitry Lovetsky (p. 9), Charlie Neibergall (p. 17); *Getty Images*: Space Frontiers (p. 17); *iStockphoto*: ©iStockphoto.com/ phdpsx (p. 30), ©iStockphoto.com/sjlocke (p. 30); *NASA*: Scott Andrews May 31, 2008 (p. 7), JSC James Blair (p. 23), NASA (pp. 5, 9, 11, 13, 15, 19, 21, 23, 27, 29), NASA May 15, 2009 (p. 11), Victor Zelentsov (p. 21); *Shutterstock*: iofoto (p. 30).

### Library of Congress Cataloging-in-Publication Data

Tieck, Sarah, 1976-
  Astronauts / Sarah Tieck.
    p. cm. -- (Extreme jobs)
  ISBN 978-1-61783-024-2
  1. Astronautics--Vocational guidance--Juvenile literature. 2. Astronauts--Juvenile literature. I. Title.
  TL850.T54 2012
  629.450092--dc23
                        2011017448

# CONTENTS

# SPACE TRAVEL 101

People have always been curious about outer space. They want to learn more about the planets, the sun, and the stars. Astronauts fly spacecraft and work in outer space.

Astronauts go to faraway places, such as the moon. What they learn helps change science. Now that's an extreme job!

In space, astronauts can see stars and planets. And, they can see Earth turning below.

# BLAST OFF!

Astronauts fly to space in spacecraft. Spacecraft connect to huge rockets and blast off into space.

Once astronauts are on board and ready, a final countdown begins. During liftoff, fire shoots out of the rockets! Smoke surrounds the spacecraft. The rockets roar as the spacecraft heads toward space.

**FACT ALERT**

Inside some rockets, temperatures can reach 6,000°F (3,300°C). Water boils at just 212°F (100°C)!

People can watch a spacecraft lift off.
They watch from a safe viewing spot.

Inside the spacecraft, a commander or **pilot** astronaut directs the flight. Astronauts wear headsets. They use these to talk and listen to each other.

Some astronauts work on the ground with mission control. From Earth, mission control helps the spacecraft's crew.

Mission control uses computers to make sure a flight goes smoothly.

Liftoff is very loud! Special headsets let astronauts talk to each other over the noise.

# GEARING UP

A spacecraft is powerful and sturdy to keep astronauts safe. To leave the spacecraft, astronauts wear special suits.

Space suits keep astronauts from getting too hot or too cold. They also allow them to breathe. People could not survive in space without spacecraft and space suits.

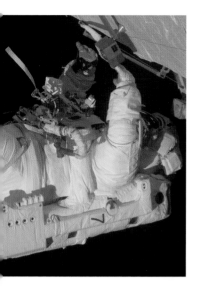

Space suits are white to stand out in the blackness of space.

Astronauts have strong helmets to cover their heads. Inside, parts let them breathe, talk, and drink.

The cockpit is where the pilot sits. He or she uses many tools to direct the spacecraft.

# Moon Walk

Groups of astronauts go to space to work on certain jobs, or missions. Crews may be in space for hundreds of days! Some astronauts are mission specialists. They plan the crew's daily work.

A crew's mission often includes science experiments. Astronauts work in labs on their spacecraft or on a space station. They study how things from Earth change in space.

The International Space Station is a space science lab shared by many countries.

Astronauts usually stay inside spacecraft. But sometimes, they work outside in space. They help build things, such as space stations. Working outside in space can be unsafe. Astronauts must be very careful!

Outside a spacecraft, astronauts could rip their space suits or drop a tool. This could hurt them or harm their spacecraft.

15

# FLOATING IN SPACE

The force of **gravity** is very different in a moving spacecraft. Everything floats as if it is weightless. So, many things are specially made for use in space. This includes beds, toilets, and food.

Astronauts eat ready-made food.
They pick their meals before their trip.

Astronauts sleep in beds or sleeping
bags that hold them in place.
Sometimes, they even sleep standing up!

Being weightless can make it very hard to do anything! So, it takes awhile for astronauts to do everyday tasks well. They may practice for months.

Before a mission, astronauts spend time training in water tanks. People float in space much like they float in water. So, astronauts practice their work in water.

**FACT ALERT**

Astronauts must exercise to keep their bodies strong. They lose strength while floating in space.

# READY, SET, GO!

**FACT ALERT**

Astronauts practice by riding in planes known as Vomit Comets. They feel what it is like to be weightless. The movement can make people sick!

In the United States, people apply at **NASA** to be astronauts. They must have a math or science **degree**. Most also have advanced degrees.

Very few who apply are chosen to go through training. Those chosen are strong and healthy. They have special skills or talents. And, they have shown they will be able to handle space travel.

It isn't easy to be in space.
So, astronauts must be fit.
They must also be comfortable
in small spaces!

During training, astronauts prepare for space travel. They take classes on space science and advanced math. They learn how to operate spacecraft. And, they learn how to live and work in space.

Astronauts practice space travel in machines called flight simulators. Inside, they have conditions similar to space. Practicing in them helps astronauts stay safe once they are in space.

Simulators have controls just like real spacecraft.

NASA's astronaut basic training program takes place at Johnson Space Center in Houston, Texas. It lasts two years. Then, astronauts begin training for missions.

23

# THEN TO NOW

On April 12, 1961, Yuri Gagarin of the Soviet Union became the first person to travel in space. His flight lasted nearly two hours and he circled Earth once.

Alan Shepard Jr. was the first American in space. He made a 15-minute flight on May 5, 1961.

On June 16, 1963, Soviet Valentina Tereshkova became the first woman in space. She spent almost three days circling Earth.

Yuri Gagarin

Valentina Tereshkova

Alan Shepard Jr.

Later missions sent astronauts outside spacecraft. On July 20, 1969, Americans Neil Armstrong and Buzz Aldrin became the first people to walk on the moon! They traveled there on *Apollo 11*.

Early spacecraft could only be used once. Then, **NASA** created spacecraft that could be used more than once. They were called space shuttles. Starting in 1981, NASA began sending them into space.

**FACT ALERT**

Many of NASA's spacecraft lift off from Kennedy Space Center in Cape Canaveral, Florida.

Buzz Aldrin (*left*) and Neil Armstrong brought moon rocks back to Earth. Scientists studied the rocks.

# BACK TO EARTH

When they aren't in space, some astronauts are preparing for their next trip. They learn new skills for missions. Other astronauts work on the ground to improve space travel or study space. Their extreme work changes science and the world!

Knowledge and training help astronauts safely do their jobs.

# WHEN I GROW UP...

**Explore parts of an astronaut's job now!**

Being an astronaut is hard on the body. So, it is important to stay healthy. Exercise and eat right so your body grows strong!

Astronauts are scientists. To live and work in space, they must know science and math. Study these subjects to strengthen your skills!

Astronauts train in water. You can practice your space skills by becoming a strong swimmer.

# IMPORTANT WORDS

**degree** a title given by a college, university, or trade school to its students for completing their studies. An advanced degree, such as a master's or a doctorate, is earned by completing graduate school after college.

**gravity** a natural force that pulls toward the center of a space object. It also pulls space objects toward each other.

**NASA** National Aeronautics and Space Administration. NASA is run by the US government to study Earth, our solar system, and outer space.

**pilot** someone whose job is to direct a ship, an airplane, or a spacecraft.

# WEB SITES

To learn more about astronauts, visit ABDO Publishing Company online. Web sites about astronauts are featured on our Book Links page. These links are routinely monitored and updated to provide the most current information available.

## www.abdopublishing.com

# INDEX